DESSA R

A New Musical

Based on the Novel by Sherley Anne Williams

Rachel York, Norm Lewis and LaChanze (left to right bottom row), and Company

Originally Produced by Lincoln Center Theatre

"DESSA ROSE" Original Cast Recording is available on Jay Records.

Project Manager: **Donna Salzburg**
Book Art Layout: **Olivia Darvas Novak**
Cover Photograph: **Brigitte LaCombe**
Interior Photographs: **Joan Marcus**, Pg. 84 **Lynn Ahrens**

WARNER BROS. PUBLICATIONS
A Warner Music Group Company
USA: 15800 NW 48th Avenue, Miami, FL 33014

INTERNATIONAL MUSIC PUBLICATIONS LIMITED
ENGLAND: GRIFFIN HOUSE,
161 HAMMERSMITH ROAD, LONDON W6 8BS

Rachel York

LaChanze

Michael Hayden

CONTENTS

WE ARE DESCENDED

Lyrics by
LYNN AHRENS

Music by
STEPHEN FLAHERTY

We Are Descended - 8 - 1
PFM0507

F
Gm7
Fm/A♭
D♭7
C7sus
wom - en.
wom - en.
Dm
F7/C
B♭
cresc.
D♭maj13
B♭/C
Wom - en.
Wom - en.
F
WOMEN:
F/E♭
Dm7
D♭maj7
E♭(9)
And we are hand-ing you down a sto - ry. Lis - ten, child, to a
MEN:
And we are hand-ing you down a sto - ry. Lis - ten, child, to a
f

F
F/E♭
B♭(9)/D
B♭9/D
D♭maj7
E♭9
sto - ry soon be yours to tell.
sto - ry soon be yours to tell.
F
F/E♭
Dm
F/C
Dm
One long gone summer of blood and glo - ry and hell.
One long gone summer of blood and glo - ry and hell.
C♯9(♭5)
Gm7/C
C
F7sus
Seem as if it all
Seem as if it all
cresc.

B♭(9)
ALL: (except DESSA ROSE + RUTH)
F(9)/A
hap-pened on - ly yes - ter - day.
Still can feel the sum - mer air.
DESSA ROSE + RUTH:
Years just up and melt a - way
Dm7
Gm7
div. 1/2 M:
C7sus
In the dis - tance I still hear some-one pick - ing out a
al - most like I still was there.
And I hear some-one pick - ing out a
C/D
Dm
Cm7
Cm7/F
B♭(9)
ban - jar tune.
DESSA ROSE:
ban - jar tune. Now, hon - ey, come and let me braid your hair.

RUTH:
F(9)/A
Dm
ALL WOMEN:
Hon - ey, have a chair, 'cause I'll be pass - ing o - ver soon and this must
ALL MEN:
I'll be pass - ing o - ver soon and this must
F/G
G7
B♭m6
B♭m6/D♭
D
nev - er pass from liv - ing mem - 'ry. Oh,
nev - er pass from liv - ing mem - 'ry. Oh,
cresc.
G
G/F
Em7
E♭maj7
F(9)
div.
we are hand-in' you down the sto - ry. Lis - ten, child, as the
div.
we are hand-in' you down the sto - ry. Lis - ten, child, as the

G
G/F
C(9)/E
C9/E
E♭maj7
F9
mu - sic of a mem - o - ry flows.
mu - sic of a mem - o - ry flows.
G
G/F
Em7
C2
Two wom - en trav - el - in' on to glo - ry...
Two wom - en trav - el - in' on to glo - ry...
Faster (𝅗𝅥 = 92)
D5
D7sus
D5
D6/9
D5
D7sus
D5
D6/9
unis.
A
f

D5
D7sus
D5
D6/9
div.
D5
D7sus
wom - an named Des - sa
Rose.
Ruth and Des - sa
unis.
div.
A wom-an named Ruth.
A

D5
D6/9
D5
D/C Cmaj7 D/A
N.C.
Rose.
A wom - an
named Des - sa
wom - an named Ruth.
A wom - an
named Des - sa
ff
f

D5
D7sus
D5
D6/9
D5
D7sus
D5
D6/9
Rose!
Rose!

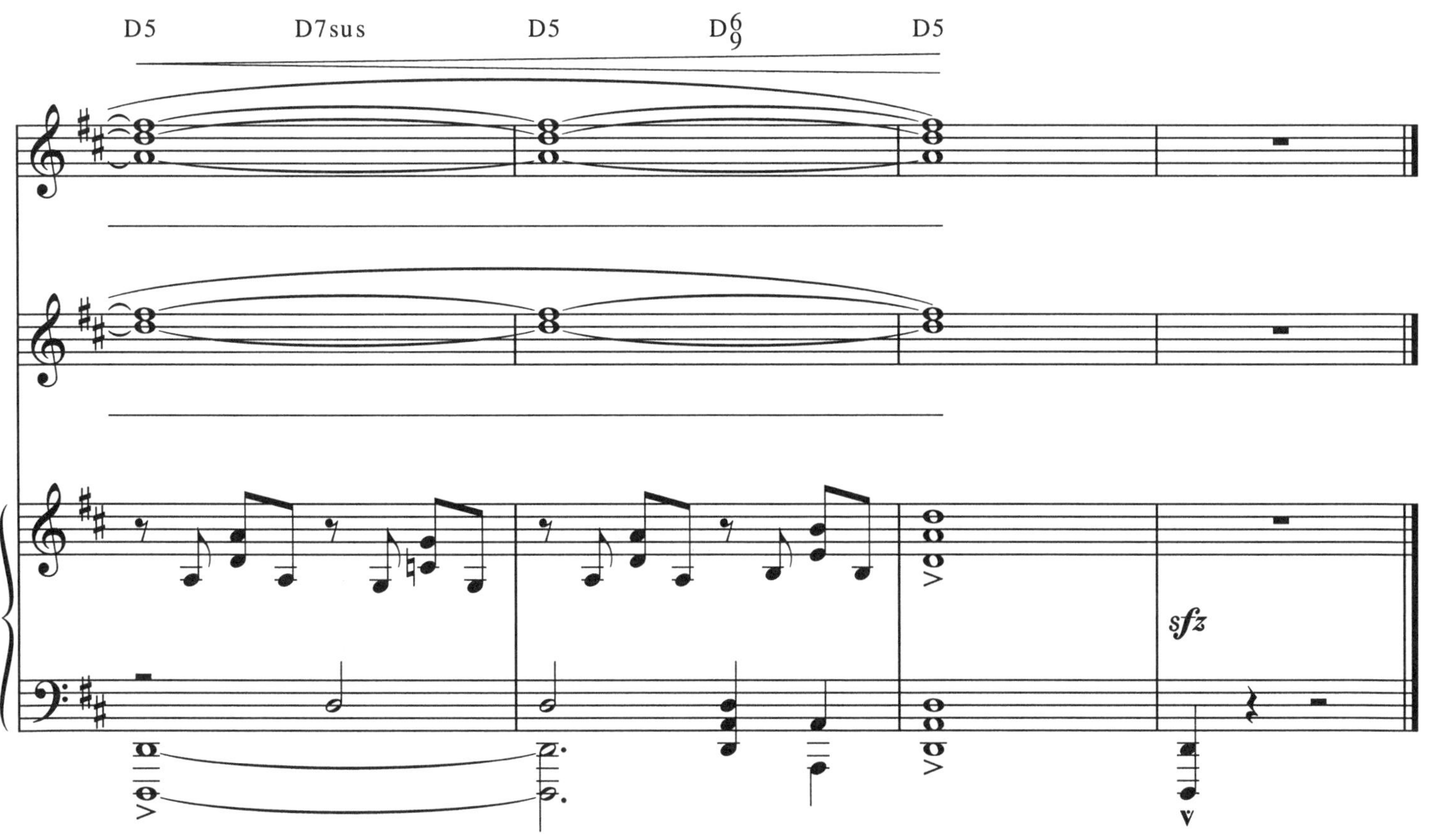
D5
D7sus
D5
D6/9
D5
sfz

OLD BANJAR

Lyrics by
LYNN AHRENS

Music by
STEPHEN FLAHERTY

Moderato (𝅗𝅥 = 80)

F♯5 B B/A♯

KAINE:

First time I ev - er hear a ban - jar play

mf

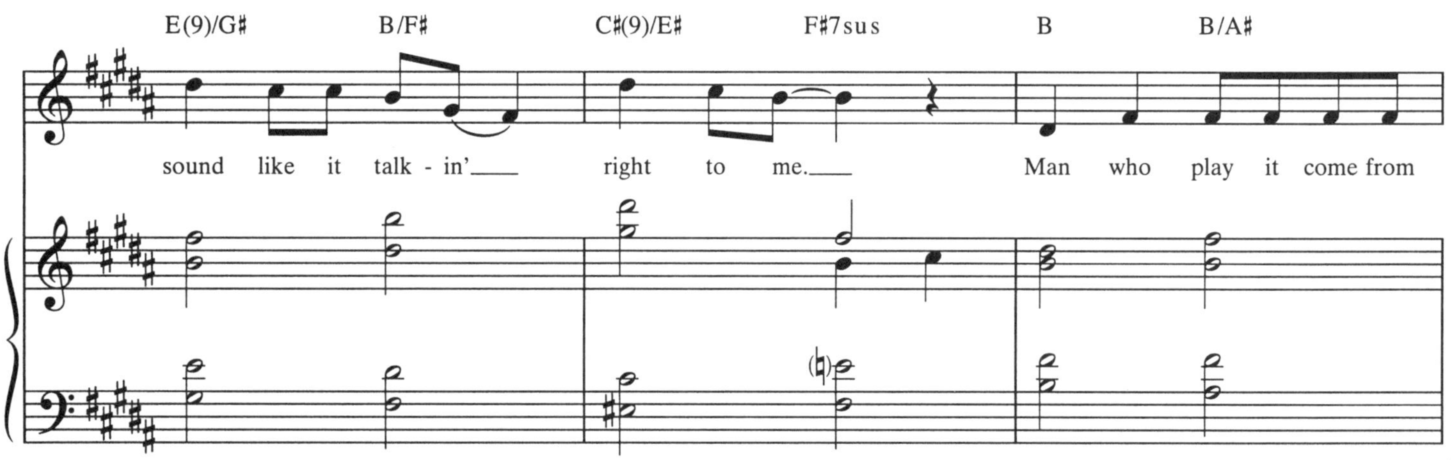

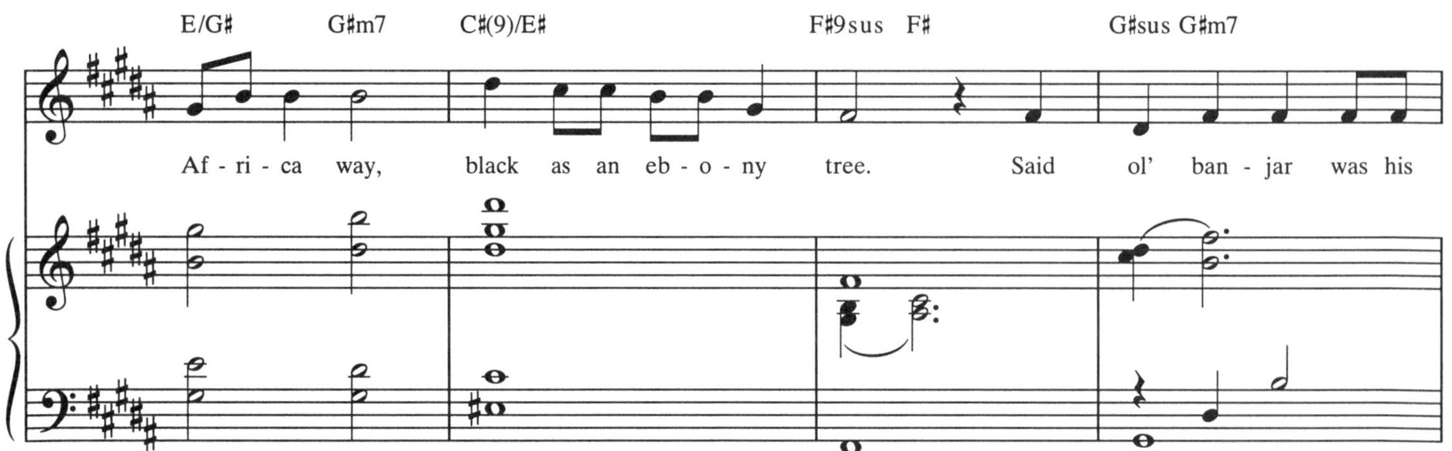

E(9)
G♯sus G♯m7
E7
home on earth, brought from an Af - ri - ca lost and gone.
G♯sus G♯m7 G♯m/F♯ G♯m C♯(9)/E♯
On - liest thing he had of worth was mu - sic to car - ry him
colla voce
Piu mosso
F♯5 F♯7sus F♯5 F♯6/9 F♯5 F♯7sus F♯7 B
on… Ain't no
a tempo
E6/9 G♯m11 E6/9 G♯m9 B/D♯
white folks down in Af - ri - ca. Ain't no white folks near or far. You
f

E6/9
F♯9sus
G♯m(9)
G♯m
C♯m
A
own your - self and you own your soul and the mu - sic of ol' ban -
F♯sus
F♯
B
B/D♯
E6/9
G♯9sus
B/D♯
jar. I want to give my Des - sa some - thin' no one
E6/9
F♯9sus
D♯m
white can take a - way...
A
colla voce
Relaxed tempo (𝅗𝅥 = 72)
E(9)
G♯m/D♯
G♯m
lit - tle piece of Af - ri - ca, a lit - tle home on earth, a
mp

C♯m7
B/D♯
A maj9
lit - tle tune on ol' ban - jar.
Send us north some
poco rit.
colla voce
E2
B/D♯
G♯m7
day.
a tempo
A bit slower, tenderly
E5
F♯5
A♭5
A♭7sus
Hey - hey, hey - hey...
mp
a tempo
A♭5
A♭5
A♭7sus
A♭5
poco rit.

SOMETHING OF MY OWN

Lyrics by
LYNN AHRENS

Music by
STEPHEN FLAHERTY

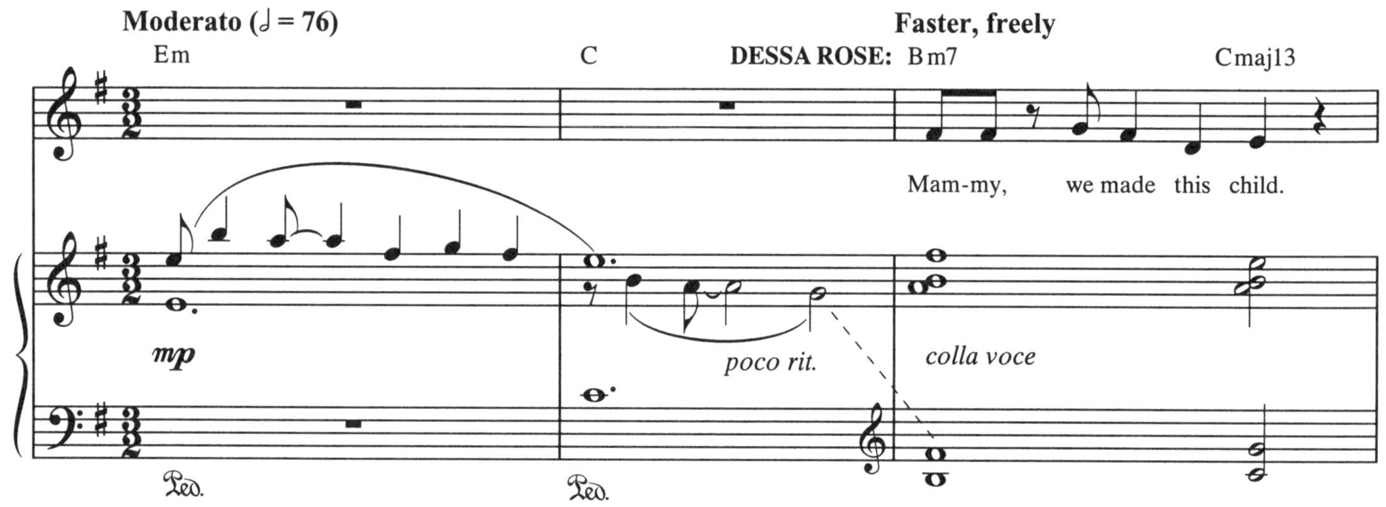

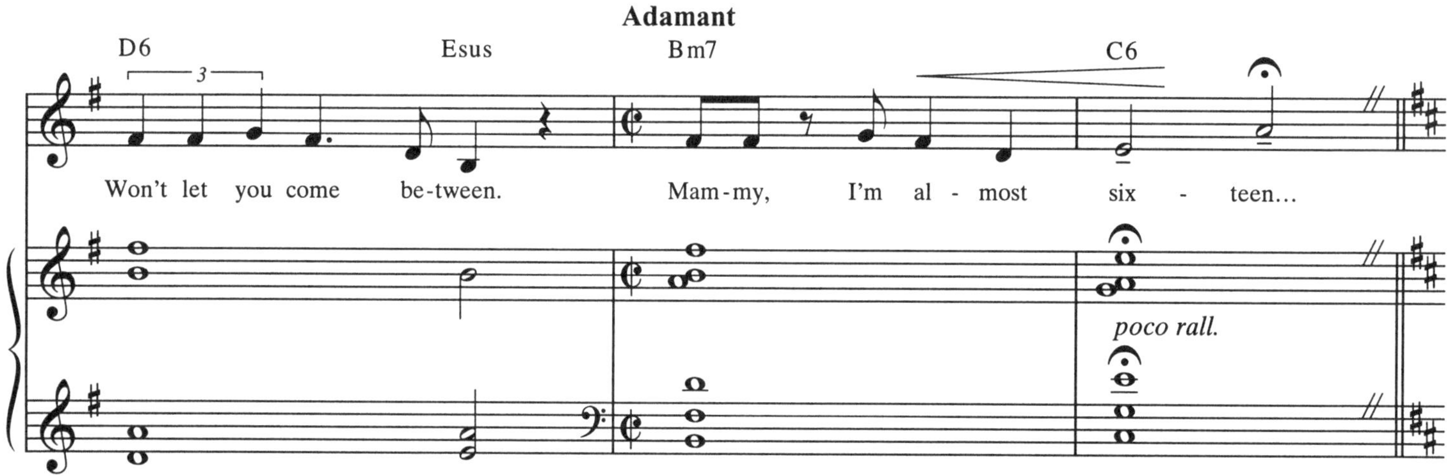

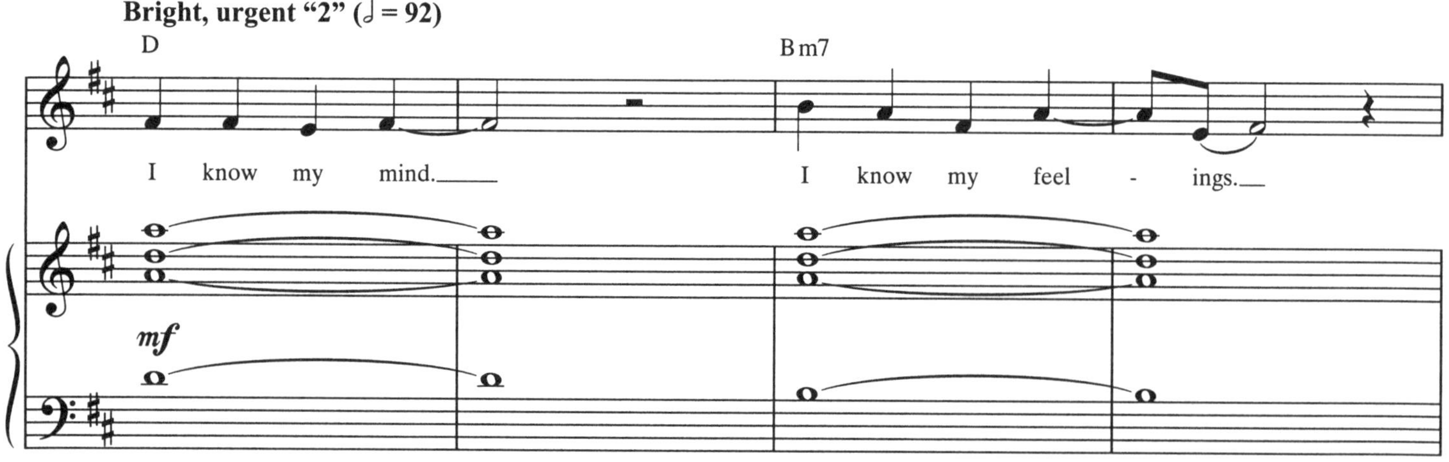

G6/9
G(9)
D2
D
Sure of my-self in ev-'ry bone.
Bm
F♯m7
Gmaj7
Bm
I got this child in - side me
Em11
G(9)/B
and it's some-thing of my own.
(roll down)
A11/C♯
G(9)/B
A/C♯
A

D
D2
D
Bm7
Un - der my heart
I feel him flut -
Bm11
Bm7
G2
G6/9
G2
ter.
Ten - der - est thing
I've ev - er
D
D2
D
D(9)
D
Bm
A/B
Bm
known.
Seem like this child
F♯m7
Gmaj7
Bm
un - tied me,

Em11
D
D2
D
gave me some - thing of my own.
(roll down)
cresc.
D2
D
cresc.
G2
D2
D
I could be as strong as thun - der with his hand in mine.
f
(Hard strum)
G2
D2
D
Tear the ver - y storm a - sun - der, make the sun to shine.

F♯m7
A/B
Bm7
B7sus
Dmaj7/A
Teach him ev - 'ry word and won - der like you taught
G2
Gmaj9
Freely
me
and when I come to
mf
mp
F♯m11
Bm
Em11
name this ba - by...
I will on - ly name him
(roll down)
colla voce
D
D7sus
D
D7sus
D5
a tempo
free.
mf
a tempo
rit.

INK

Lyrics by
LYNN AHRENS

Music by
STEPHEN FLAHERTY

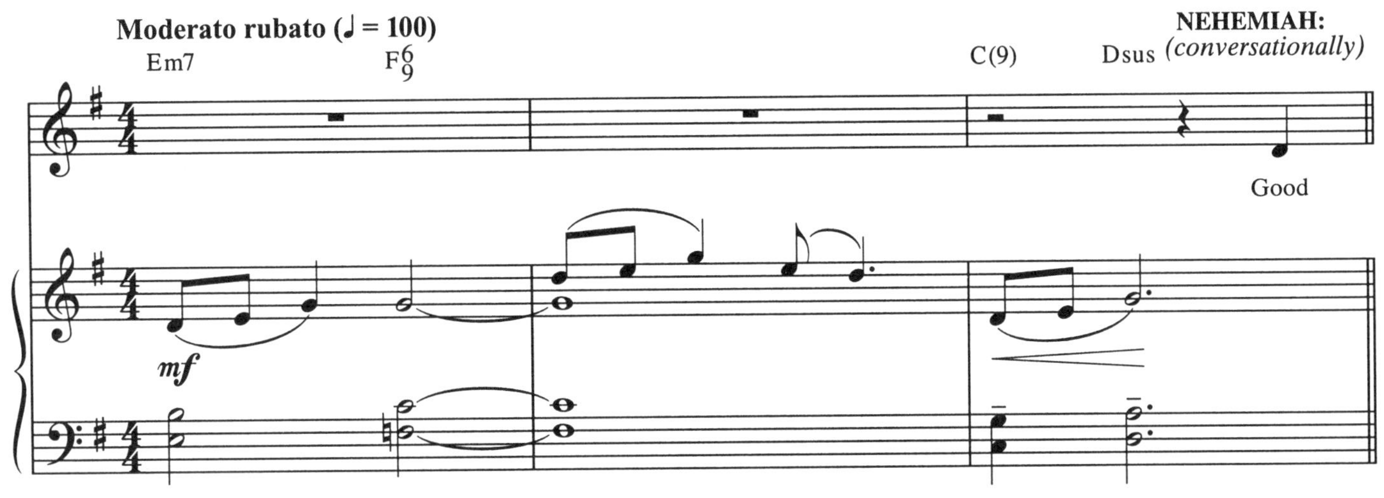

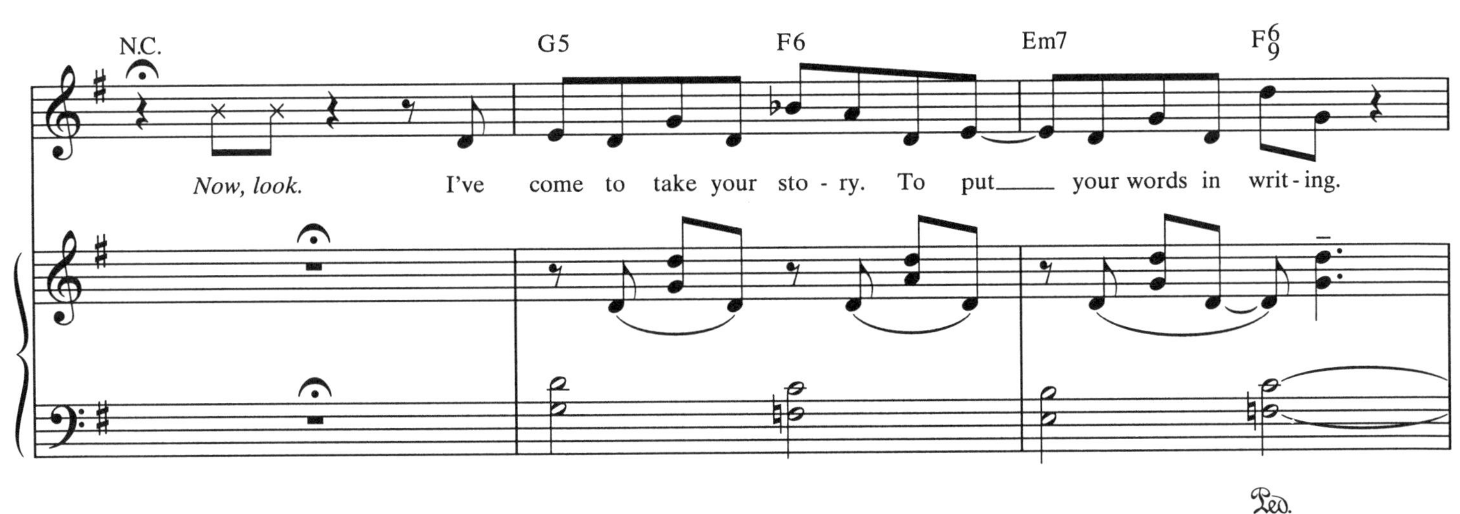

N.C.
C(9)
Dm(4)
My book is all a - bout re - bel - lion and slaves
poco a poco cresc.
E♭maj7
F6/9
F6/A
G
Am(4)
C9
who run a - way. The slaves who kill their mas - ters.
f
N.C.
mp
G
Am11
B♭6
C(9)
I've got all day.
mp
Em7
F6/9
C(9)
Dsus
Now

G5
F6/9
listen here, O - dessa.
G5
F6
Your story is important.
mf
N.C.
G5
F6
Em7
F6/9
Come, come. A woman on a cofle, who leads a slave rebellion...
poco a poco cresc.
Ped.
N.C.
C(9)
Dm(4)
Don't hum! I've interviewed some others but you're
poco a poco cresc.
E♭maj7
F6/9
F6/A
G
Am(4)
C9
the real prize. They call you devil woman...
molto cresc.
f
mf
7

Bm C D7sus Em7 A7 C7
This here is pa - per. Ink goes on the pa - per. Lasts e - ven af -
C(9) E♭7 G Bm C D7sus Em7
ter you're gone. I'll write your words and they'll last for -
A7 C7 N.C. G Am11
ev - er… Time's tick - in' on.
mp
ff
cresc.
f
B♭6 C(9) Em7 F2 C(9) Dsus
I'm

G5
F6/9
asking you, O - des - sa.
G5
F6
For his - to - ry, O - des - sa.
mf
(More deliberate)
N.C.
Just think.
You're
G
on your way to
F6
glo - ry. So leave
poco a poco cresc.
Em7
poco rit.
F6/9
your child your sto - ry...
In
poco rit.
G5
F6
Em7
F6
G5
ink.
mf
poco rit.

LITTLE STAR

Lyrics by
LYNN AHRENS

Music by
STEPHEN FLAHERTY

A5
Em7
A5
Em(9)
Give your friends a wish to-night.
Lit - tle star,
shin-ing bright,
give your friends a wish to-night.
A5
Em7
A5
Em9 A7sus
Wish we might be free.
Wish we may be free.
D2
BOTH:
N: div.
H:
And we'll go danc - in' in the sky,

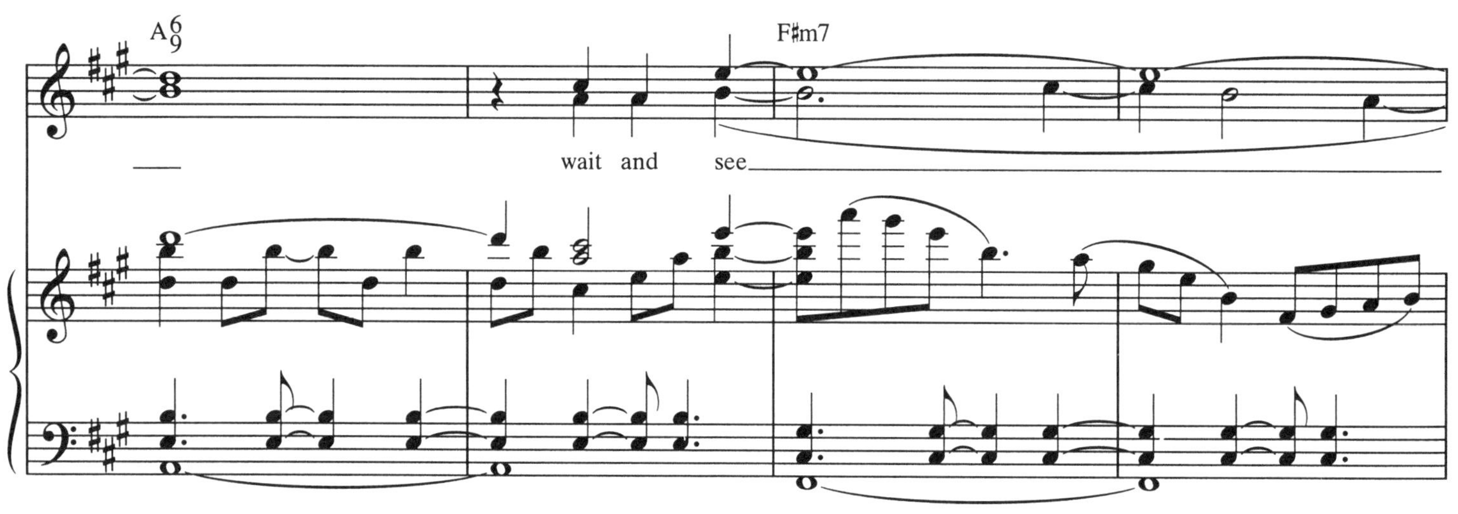
A6/9
F♯m7
wait and see

D2
NATHAN:
when we're
poco a poco cresc.

G(9)
(NATHAN:)
cresc.
E7sus
E5
free...
HARKER:
When we're free...
molto cresc.

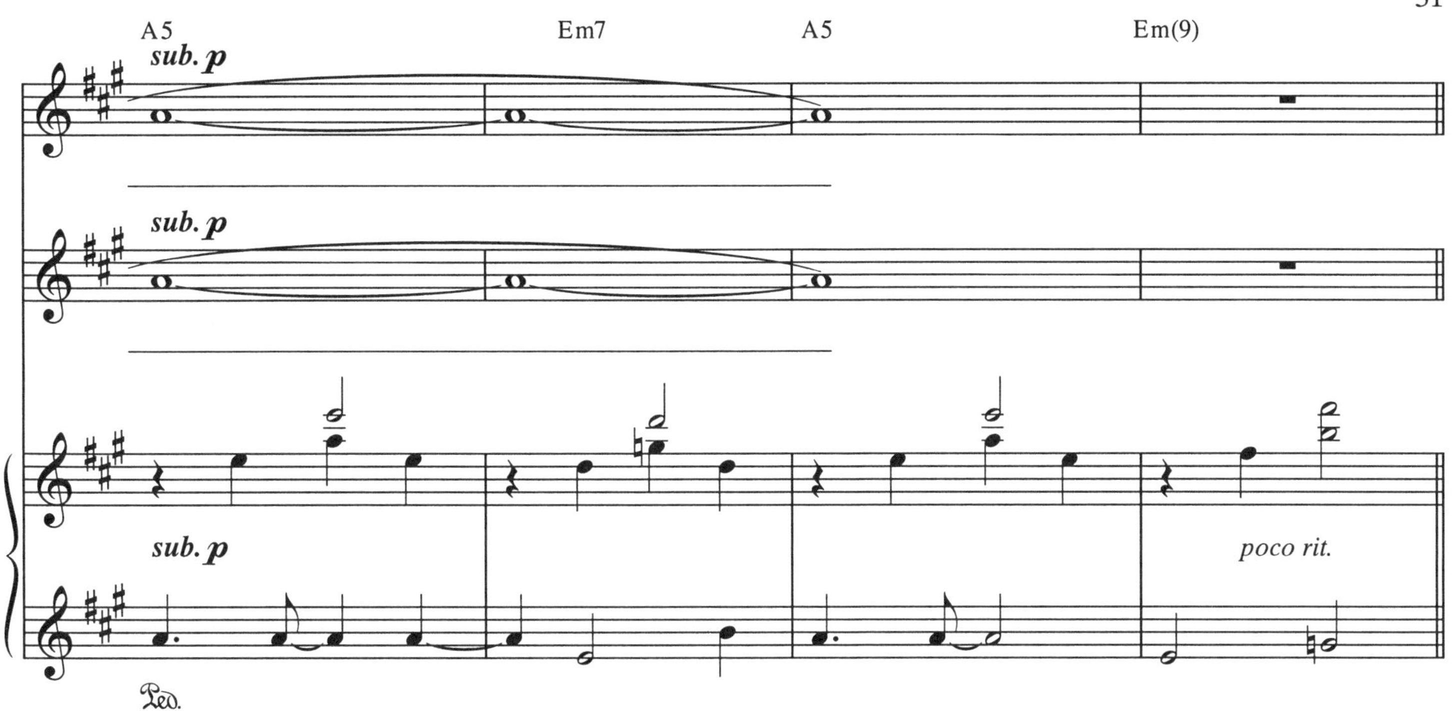
A5
Em7
A5
Em(9)
sub. p
sub. p
sub. p
poco rit.

Slower, more freely
D5
A5
a tempo
NATHAN:
HARKER:
BOTH:
Wish we may,
wish we might
be
free…
a tempo

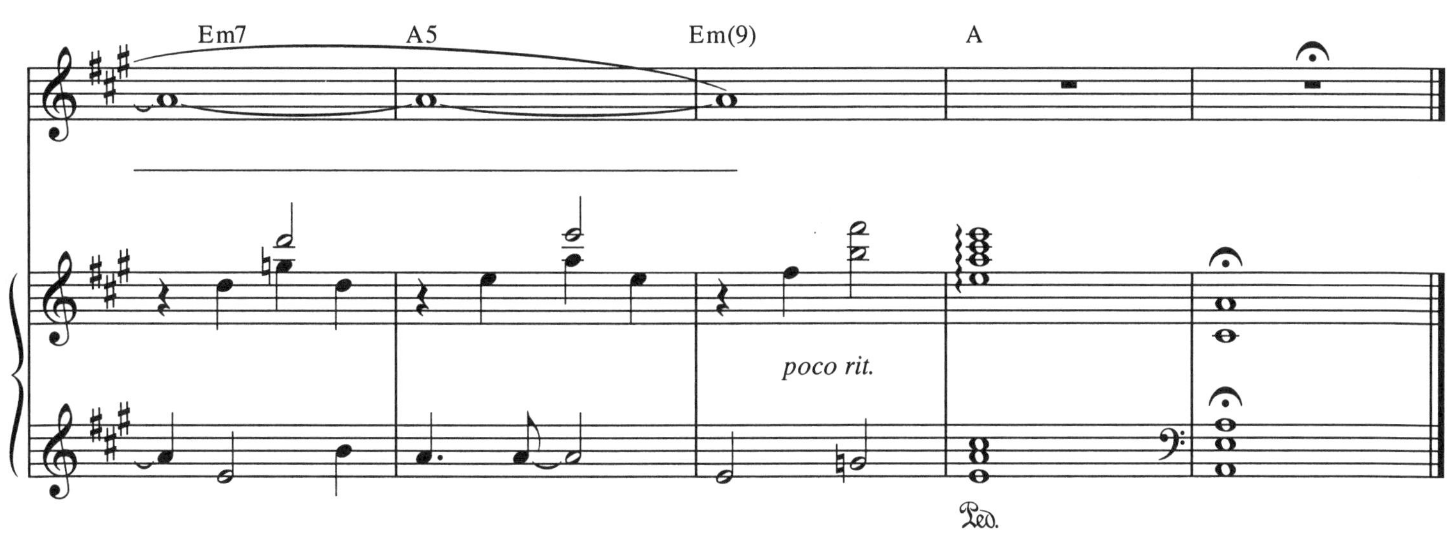
Em7
A5
Em(9)
A
poco rit.

AT THE GLEN

Lyrics by
LYNN AHRENS

Music by
STEPHEN FLAHERTY

Simple, hymn-like (♩ = 66)

RUTH: *Wednesday at the Glen. Dear Bertie, I write you yet another letter in my mind as there seems to be no better way to contact you.*

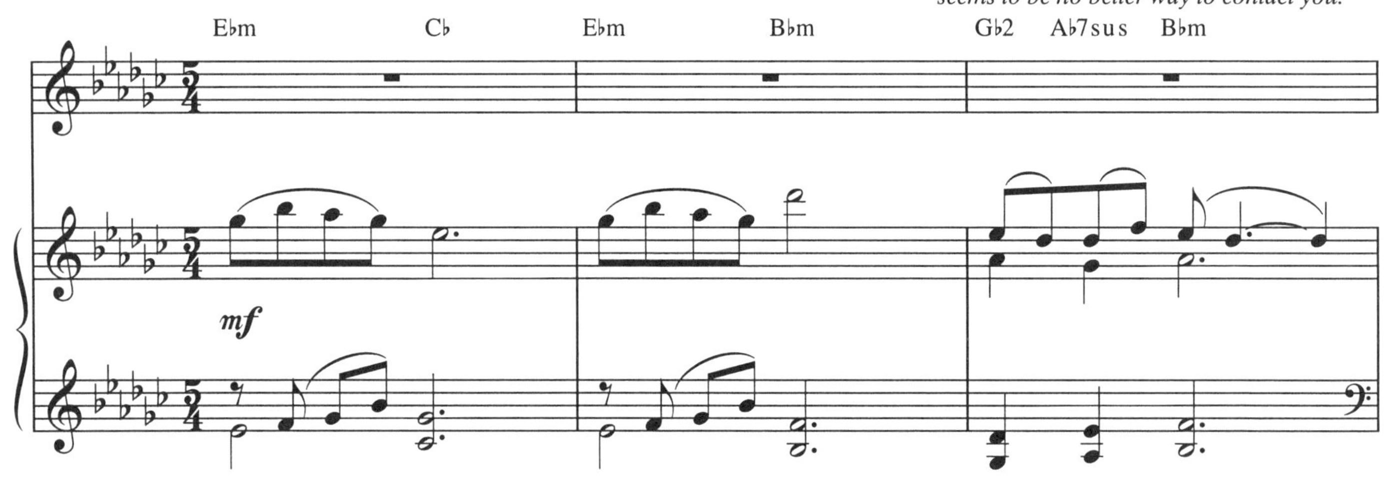

Cbmaj7
Fb6
Bbm
Gb(9)
Charles - ton, Ber - tie? Things gone on these sev - en months. Well,
Bbm
Fm
Gb2
Absus
Bbm
things have gone too far. Mam-my died at Christ-mas, so
Fm
Gb(9)
Gb
Db
Ab
Gbmaj7
Gb/Ab
Fm
sud - den, Ber-tie. And ev - 'ry week new nig - ras come here, I don't
Gb(9)
Absus
Bbm
Gb
Ebm7/Ab
Bbm
know from where. May - be some of them are run - a - ways who heard the

C♭
G♭/B♭
A♭7sus
N.C.
G♭(9)
mas-ter's nev-er there. You been gone these sev - en months. Don't you
mf
B♭m7
Fm7
B♭2
C♭2(♯11)
miss me now and then? Oh, Ber - tie, it's so lone - some at the Glen.
poco rit.
Moderately (♩ = 120)
(Ruth digresses, dreamily.)
D
I
mp
Ped.
of - ten think of Charles - ton, our sea - son in Charles - ton, when

Amaj7
F♯m
we were in - vi - ted all o - ver the cit - y and
D
poco rall.
Mam - my would fuss and I al - most felt pret-ty and
poco rall.
D♭
D♭/F
G♭(9)
G♭/F
look at me now as I climb up the stair: Your
Ped. throughout
E♭m7
E♭m7/A♭
D♭
stair - case to no - where. Your grand wind - ing

D♭/F
G♭(9)
G♭
stair - case that stops in mid - air
A
B♭m/F F
B♭m/F F
E♭/D D
E♭/D D
stair - case to no - where!
Your
piu mosso
E♭7
un - fin-ished kit-chen, your farm all ne - glect-ed. The
mf
Ped.
Dm
Gm(9)
Gm
Gm/F
mas - ter who's al - ways and nev - er ex - pect-ed but

E♭7
why should I care when I've still got that
B♭+/E
stair! I
F(9 ♯11)
sub. p
step 'cross the thresh - hold and lose my breath. It's
p
Ped.
Em(9)
Am(9)
some - thing like ter-ror but more like death. I

F(9)
E♭(9)
do not go out and I sleep till noon.
Ber - tie,
A7sus(♭9)
come home soon. Ber - tie, come home soon. Come home
poco rall.
a tempo
F♯/E E F♯/E
E F♯/E
Emaj9 F♯/E
soon...
Ber - tie...
a tempo
E F♯/E E
Ber - tie... Ber - tie...

Emaj7 G♯sus N.C.

You been

Tempo primo (♩ = 66) G♭(9) B♭m D♭5/A♭ A♭

gone these sev - en months and they whis - per you ain't com - in' back a -

mp

G♭(9) G♭maj7 (no 3rd) A♭2 B♭m G♭ A♭ B♭m

gain. Oh, Ber - tie, times is hard.___ There's strang-ers in the yard.___ And,

mp

G♭2 N.C. F♭6/9 D♭

Ber - tie, it's so lone - some at the Glen.___

mf

CAPTURE THE GIRL

Lyrics by
LYNN AHRENS

Music by
STEPHEN FLAHERTY

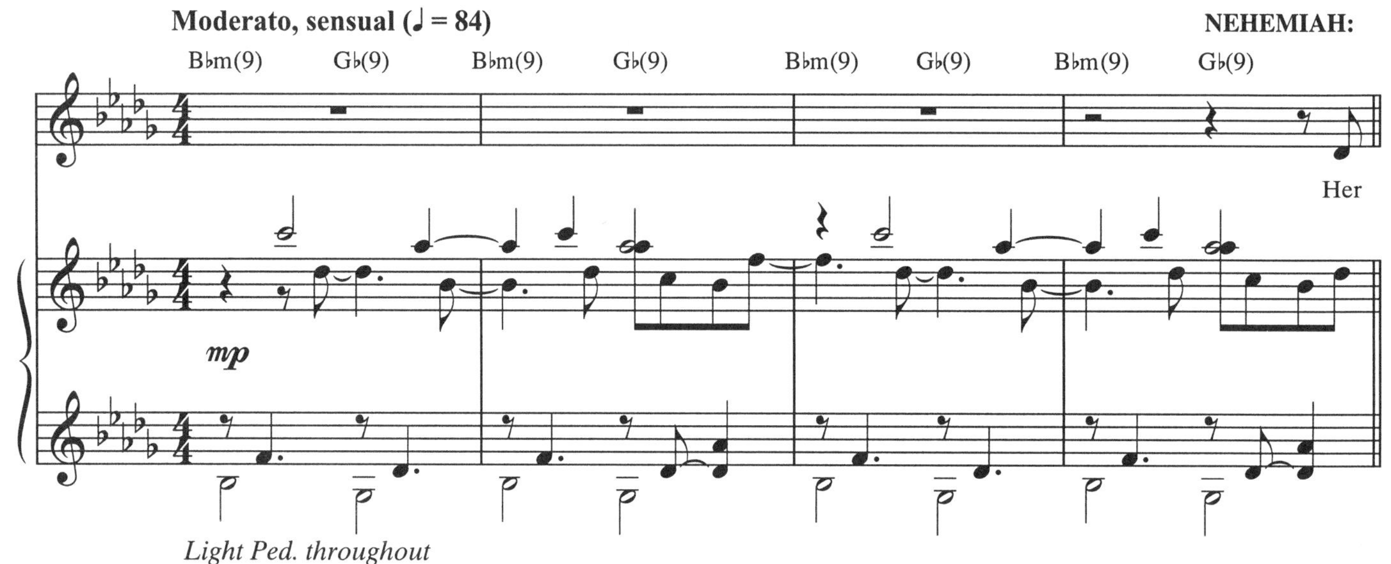

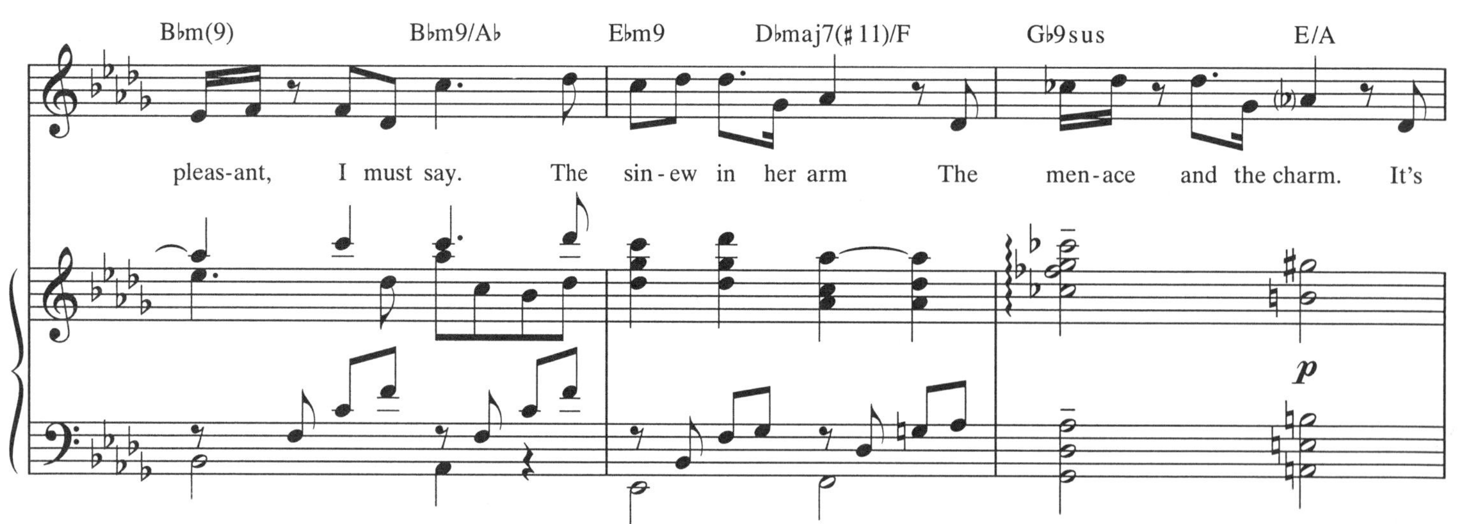

B♭m7
D♭9/A♭
G♭(9)
E/A
B♭m(9)
G♭(9)
dif-fi-cult to cap-ture the girl.
mf
B♭m(9)
G♭(9)
B♭m(9)
G♭(9)
B♭m(9)
G♭(9)
Her flash of sud-den wit can catch you un-a-ware. I
B♭m(9)
G♭(9)
B♭m(9)
B♭m9/A♭
E♭m9
D♭maj7(♯11)/F
see why some have said she has a dev-il stare. That closed and guard-ed face. That
G♭9sus
E/A
B♭m7
a tempo
D♭9/A♭
G♭(9)
G♭maj7 A♭
un-ex-pect-ed grace. So dif-fi-cult to cap-ture the girl. Is she
colla voce
p
mf a tempo
cresc.

Fm7/B♭ B♭m A♭/G♭ G♭maj9 Fm7/B♭ B♭m A♭(9)/G♭ G♭maj9 Fm7/B♭ B♭m A♭/G♭ G♭maj9
think-ing of__ her ba-by? Is she think-ing of__ her death? Is she won-d'ring what__ I'm scratch-ing in__ my
f
A♭/B♭ B♭m A♭/B♭ B♭m E♭m9 Fm7 G♭sus2 sus4 G♭(9) Fm7/A♭ B♭m7
book? Now that un-re-pen - tant glance that I no-tice just__ by chance. Does she
E♭ D♭/F E♭/G A7 B♭m(9) G♭(9)
mock me? Does she fear me? Does she hate me? Does she hear me?______
mp
B♭m(9) G♭(9) B♭m(9) G♭(9) B♭m(9) G♭(9) B♭m(9) G♭(9)
The col-umn of her neck. The
mf

B♭m(9)
G♭(9)
B♭m(9)
G♭(9)
B♭m(9)
B♭m9/A♭
sin-ew in her arm. The grav-el of her voice. The men-ace and the charm. The
E♭m9
D♭maj7(♯11)/F
G♭9sus
E/A
a tempo
B♭m7
D♭7/A♭
un-re-pen - tant stare. The glint of pe-koe tea. A pair of eyes like eb-o-ny and pearl.
mp colla voce
mf a tempo
poco a poco rit.
E♭7/G
Amaj13
D♭(9)/A♭
A7/A♭
E♭/A♭
A♭7sus
A♭7
So dif-fi-cult to sum up, to mea-sure, to cap-ture the
mp
poco a poco rit.
molto rit.
a tempo
B♭m(9)
G♭(9)
B♭m(9)
G♭(9)
B♭m(9)
girl.
a tempo
rit.

FLY AWAY

Lyrics by
LYNN AHRENS

Music by
STEPHEN FLAHERTY

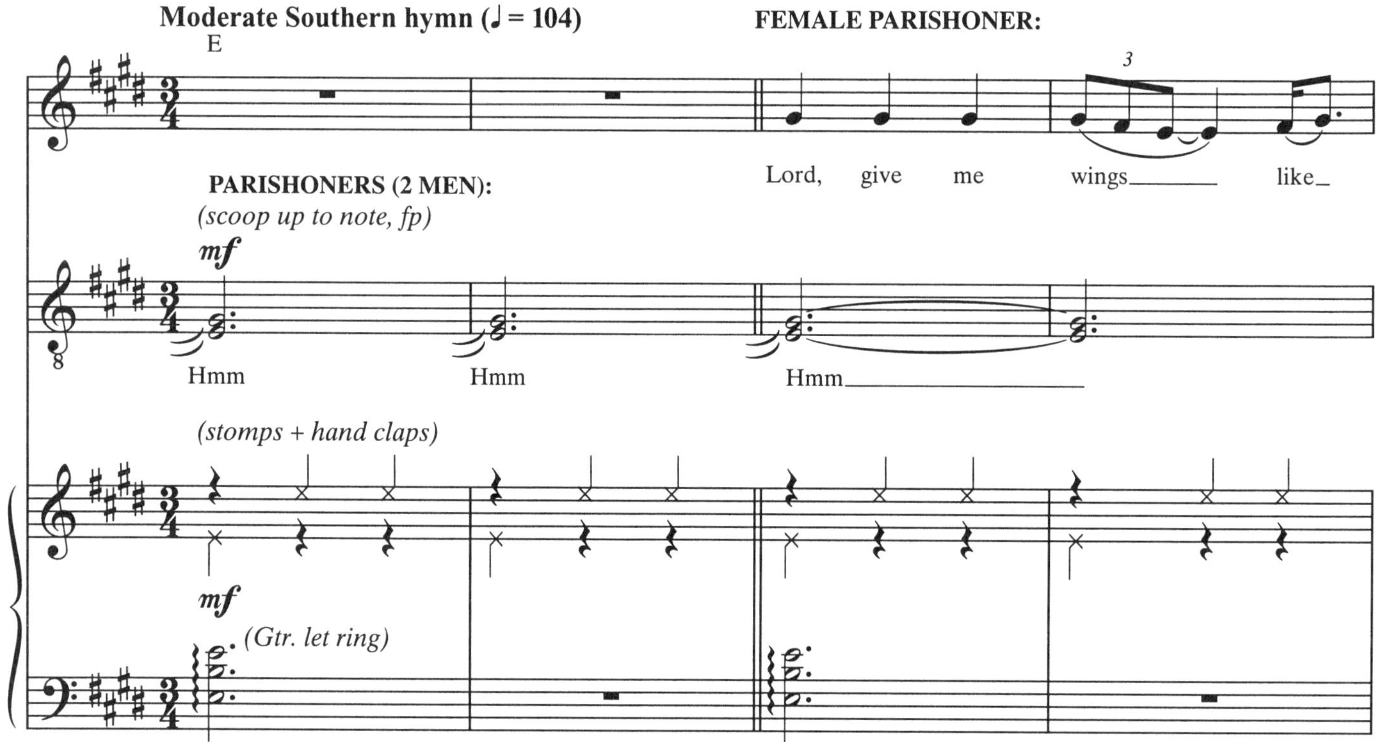

B
wings like No - ah's dove. I'll
Hmm Hmm I'll
E
A/E
fly 'cross these fields to the Lord I love.
fly 'cross these fields to the Lord I love.
E
B
E
Oh, I will fly a - way.
unis.
Oh, I will fly a - way.

E
SUSANNAH:
F♯m/E
E
A/E
Lord, give me wings like No - ah's
dolce
E
(SUSANNAH:)
Esus
E
dove.
Lord, give me wings like
M:
PARISHONERS:
(W, M:)
Lord, give me
C♯m
Bsus
B
B2
B/A
No - ah's dove.
I'll
wings.
No - ah's dove.

E/G♯ A E/D C♯m7
fly 'cross these fields to the Lord I love.
Hmm Hmm Hmm
(M1)
(M2) (Hmm) Hmm (Hmm
F♯m7(♭5)/C D9 F♯m7(♭5)/C E/B Bsus
cresc.
Oh, I will fly…
M:
M, W:
)
Oh, I will fly…
F♯ G♯m/F♯ F♯ B m/F♯ G♯m7(♭5)/F♯ B m/F♯ G♯m7(♭5)/F♯
SUSANNAH+PARISHONERS:
(S:)
DESSA ROSE:
Tell me, sis - ter.
NEHEMIAH:
Lord, give me wings like No - ah's dove.

D♯m7
Tell me, broth-er.
C♯/D♯
D♯m7
Tell me, broth-er.
B m/D
F♯/C♯
B m
G♯dim/B
B m/D♯
C♯
Oh,
cresc.
poco rall.
Jubilant
F♯
G♯m/F♯
F♯
G♯m7(♭5)/F♯
F♯
G♯m/C♯
SUSANNAH:
Lord, give me wings.
f DESSA ROSE:
Lord, give me wings like No - ah's dove. Tell me, sis - ter.
f
F♯7
G♯m/F♯
B/F♯
F♯
D♯m
Oh, Lord, give me wings like No - ah's
Tell me, broth-er.
Tell me, sis - ter.

G♯m7/C♯
B/C♯
C♯/B
F♯/A♯
Bmaj7
F♯/B
(SUSANNAH:)
dove. I'll fly 'cross these fields to the
(DESSA ROSE:)
how long will it be? Dont let a
FEMALE PARISHONER:
Hmm Hmm
2 MALE PARISHONERS:
Hmm Hmm
Emaj7
F♯/F♯
Emaj7
D♯m7
cresc.
Lord I love.
poor, poor sin - ner suf - fer one more day.
cresc.
Hmm Hmm
cresc.
Hmm Hmm
cresc.

G♯dim/D F♯/C♯ G♯dim/B B m/D C♯m B m F♯/C♯

molto cresc.

f

Oh, I will

molto cresc.

Oh, I will

molto cresc.

Hmm Oh, I will

+NEHEMIAH:

Hmm Oh, I will

molto cresc.

B/C♯ F♯/C♯ G♯dim/D F♯/C♯ G♯dim/B

fly, I will fly,

fly, I will fly,

fly, I will fly,

fly, I will fly,

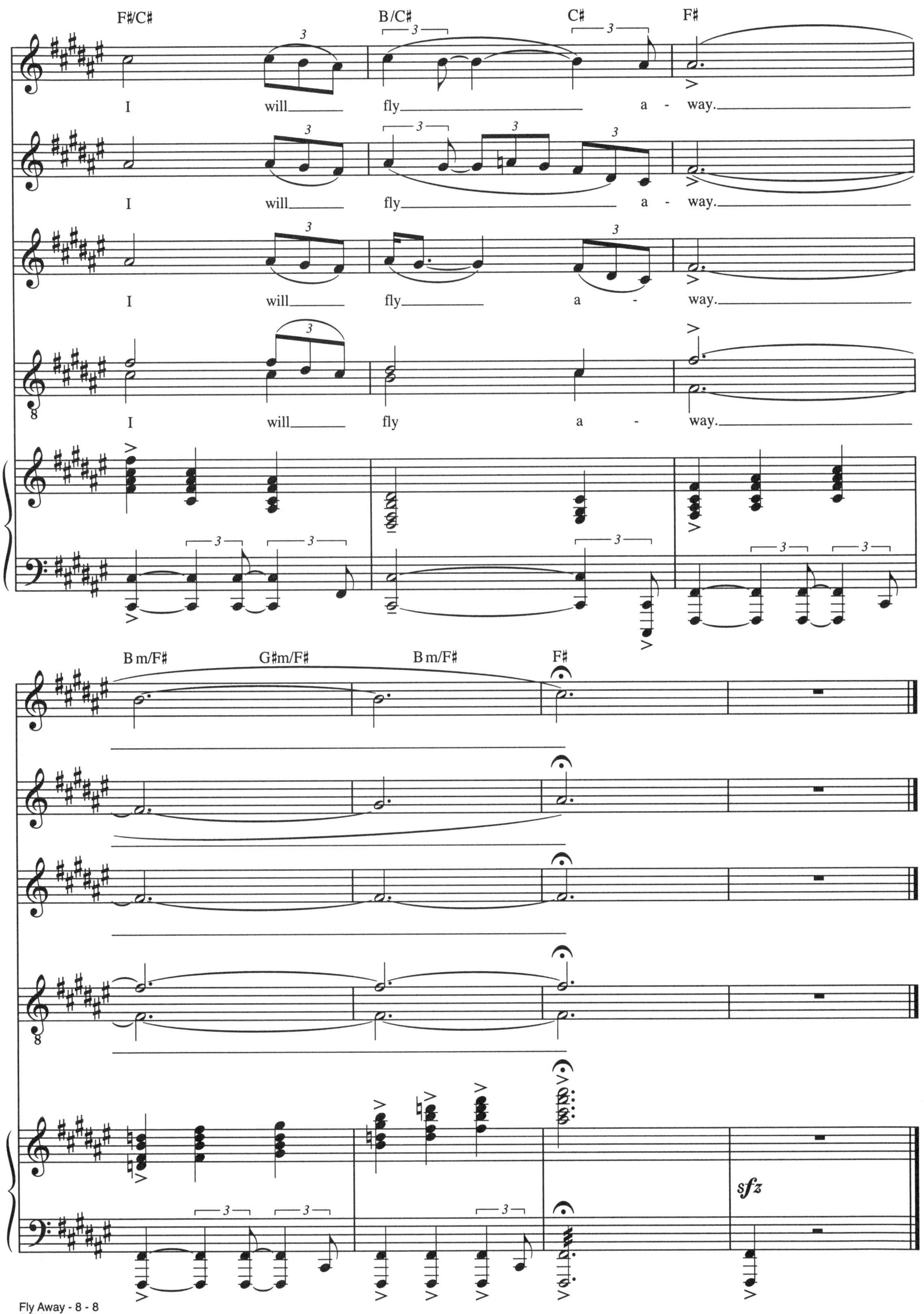
F♯/C♯
B/C♯
C♯
F♯
I will fly a - way.
I will fly a - way.
I will fly a - way.
I will fly a - way.
B m/F♯
G♯m/F♯
B m/F♯
F♯
sfz

TWELVE CHILDREN

Lyrics by
LYNN AHRENS

Music by
STEPHEN FLAHERTY

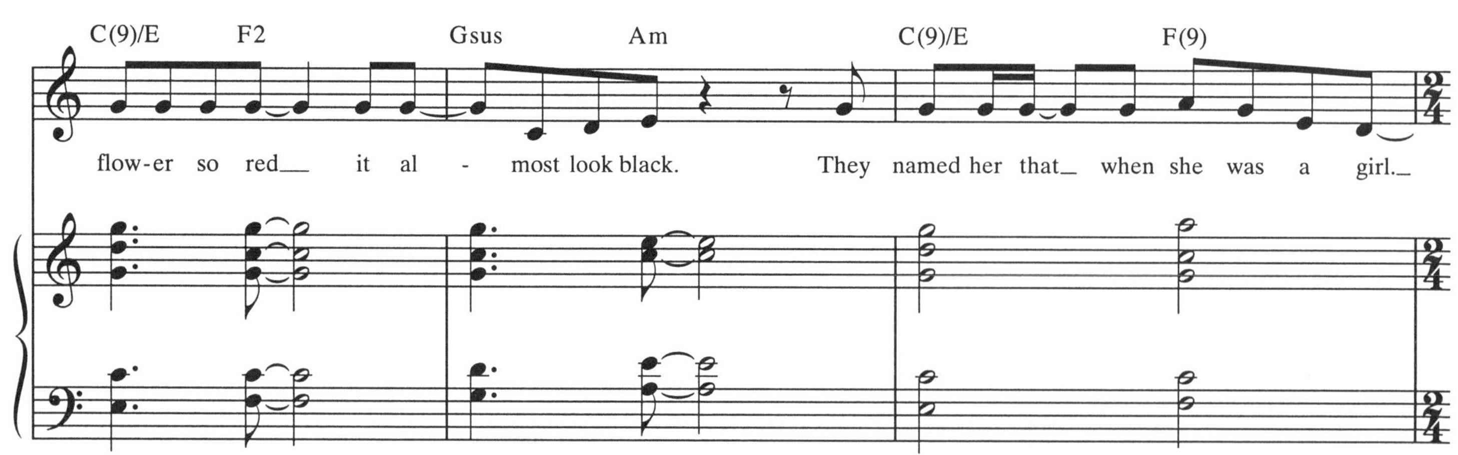

Gsus G/F C/E F2 G5 F(9)
Smooth_ and black like_ pet - als I s'pose.
G7sus C2 F2 G Am
And they teased her cause she worked_ 'round the dair - y._ Said her
Em Am C/D D F2 Am7
kiss was as tang - y as clab - ber. These_ things_ on - ly her_
F G5 C(9) Cmaj9/E F2
chil - dren_ knows. Mam - my gave birth_ to twelve_
mf

Gsus
Csus C/D
Cmaj9/E
F2
G G/A Am
children!
Twelve that come in - to this world still liv - in'. The
Cmaj9/E F2
G Am
C/B♭
first one a boy named Lit - tle Joe. Named for the mas - ter.
mp
Gsus G/F
Em F2
Gsus G Am
Sec-ond one died with - out no name.
mf
C/E Em F2
Gsus G Am
Cmaj7/E F2
White folks said it was all the same, but Mam - my called her Min-

G
Am
F(9)
ta
for re-mem - brance.
p
Ped.
Eb/Bb
F9/Bb
Abm6/Bb
Eb/Bb
F9/Bb
Seth her first child who lived to work the field.
Mar - y and Bess, then
mp
Ped. sim.
Abm6/Bb
Eb/Bb
Cm
F9
Abm6
Eb
Jess and A - mos.
All of them gone in a week one Eas - ter,
Cm
Bb(9)
Ab(9)
trad - ed for some mules.
But then come Jee - ter, the
poco rit.
colla voce

F7sus Fm7/E♭
Bbmaj7/D E♭2
F Gm
laugh-in' one!
Jee-ter, he run. Mam-my told me so.
(In Tempo)
mf
Bbmaj7/D E♭(9)
F Gm
May-be he's liv - in'. Nev - er will know. But
B♭/D E♭2
Fsus
B♭sus B♭
Freely
Gm C
Jee - ter give her hope.
Cea-sar died at the
sub. p
E♭m6
A bit slower
Gm C
E♭m6
end of a rope.
She

(Tempo I)
G A9 C9 E♭7 G Am11
lost lit - tle Jef - frey to the sting of a bee. They sold Car - rie Mae. Her
mf
C9 G C2 G/B B7/D♯ Em
last was me. I'm her on - ly ba - by whose name she chose:
cresc.
C2 D♯dim Em C(9)
"Des - sa" for "des - cen - dant" of a wom - an named Rose!
mp rit.
Slower
D5 G5 C2
Lit - tle Joe, Min - ta, Seth, A - mos, Mar - y, Jess, Bess, Jee - ter,

Em7
A7
C
G
C/D
G
Ceas - ar, Jef - frey, Car - rie Mae and Des - sa Rose. Our names is Joe, Min - ta, Seth, A - mos,
poco a poco cresc.
C2
Em7
A7
C
G
B7/F♯
Ma - ry, Jess, Bess, Jee - ter, Ceas - ar, Jef - frey, Car - rie Mae and Des - sa Rose. My own
molto cresc.
Em
B7/E
Em
C/D
selve. That make twelve.
f
poco accel.
cresc.
Deliberate (With quiet intensity and rising anger)
D
p
G5
G5/F
Em7
E♭maj7
F2
Some sold a - way. Some passed a - way. Some run. Twelve
mf
p

G5
G5/F
Em7
E♭maj7
F(9)
chil - dren brought from her bod - y, all gone but one. I
G
G/F
C/E
Em
tell these names the way my Mam - my told these names lest her poor
mf
G/A
A7
Am7(♭5)/E♭
chil - dren pass from liv - in' mem - 'ry.
Em
A7
Am7(♭5)/E♭
mp
Mmm...
Mmm...
And
p

(Tempo I)
C(9)/E
F2
Gsus
Am
you, lit - tle girl,
you fol - low in line.
Your
mp
C/E
F(9)
Gsus
G/F
Mam - my holds you safe as she can.
C/E
F2
G
Am
F(9)
One fine day we'll count you the same.
Daugh-ter, my
DESSA ROSE (spoken):
I made a promise to your daddy and your Grandmammy Rose. When we get north…
(sung:)
Dm7(♭5)/A♭
F(9)
Gsus
G
Am
D7
F(9)
Fm/A♭
C
daugh-ter,
you'll have your name.
rit.
rit.

IN THE BEND OF MY ARM

Lyrics by
LYNN AHRENS

Music by
STEPHEN FLAHERTY

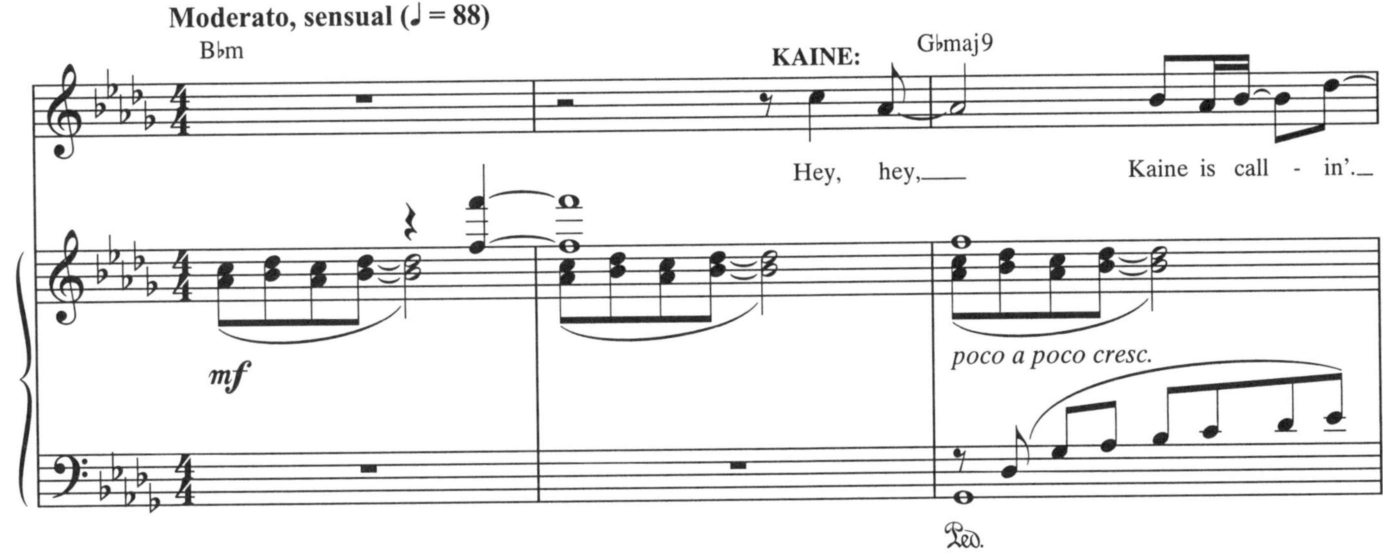

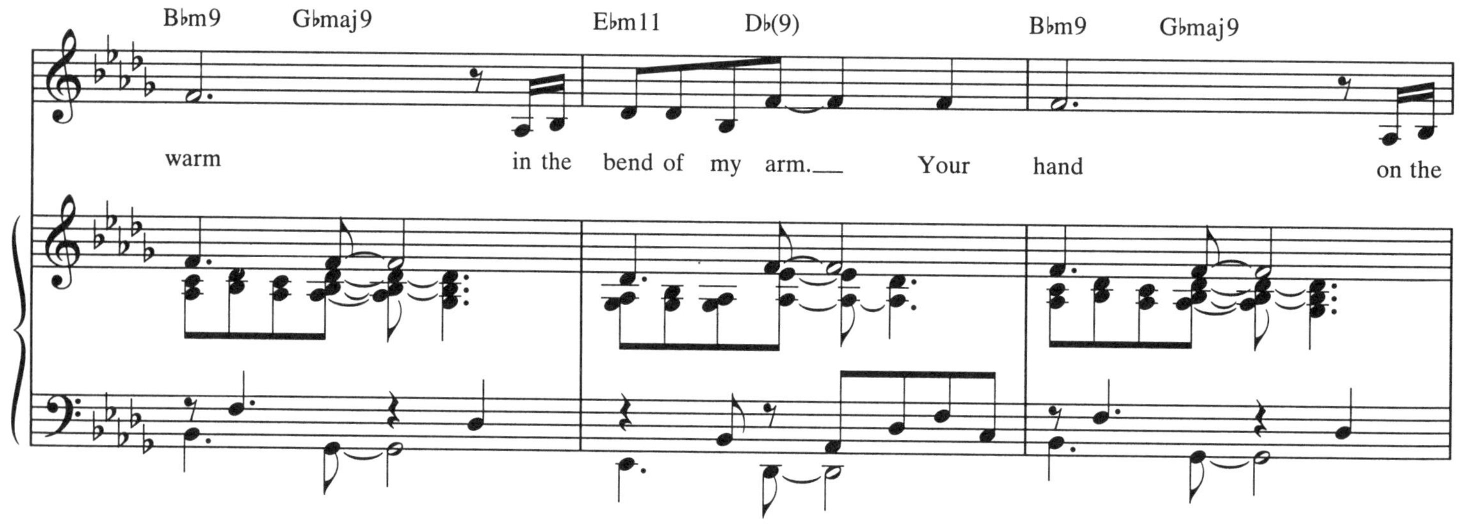
Bbm9
Gbmaj9
Ebm11
Db(9)
Bbm9
Gbmaj9
warm
in the bend of my arm.
Your hand
on the

Ebm11
Db(9)
Bbm9
Gbmaj9
Ebm11
Db(9)
hill of my bod - y.
Your lips
on the field of my breast.
Your

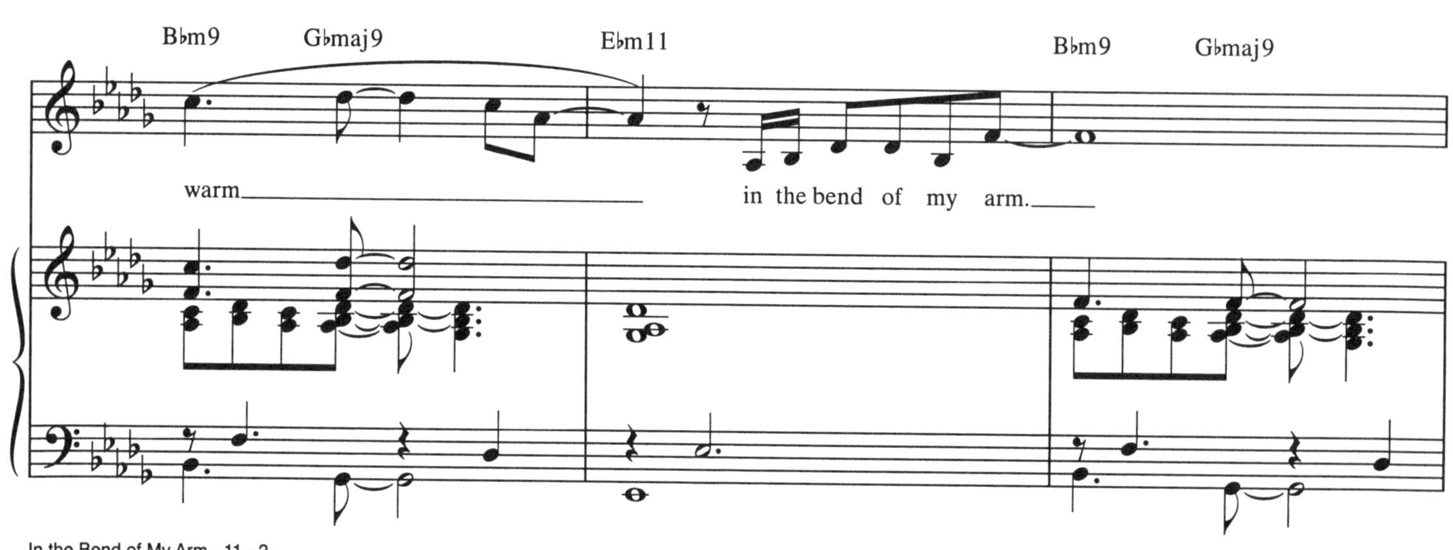
Bbm9
Gbmaj9
Ebm11
Bbm9
Gbmaj9
warm
in the bend of my arm.

Ebm11
Db(9)
(DESSA ROSE:)
Mmm....
Bbm9
Gbmaj9
KAINE:
Hey,
hey...
Your
(KAINE:)
skin
on the
tips of my fin - gers.
Your
soft
on the
side of my face.
Your
mouth
on the
slope of my shoul - der
Your
(DESSA ROSE:)
Your

B♭m9
G♭maj9
E♭m11
B♭m9
G♭maj9
warm
in the bend of my arm.
warm
in the bend of my arm.
E♭m11
D♭(9)
B♭m9
G♭maj9
E♭m11
D♭(9)
Mmm...
Mmm...
B♭sus
B♭m7
G♭6 9
B♭sus
B♭m7
Taste like rain.
Smell like earth.
Taste like rain.
Smell like earth.
f

G♭6/9
C♭maj13
B♭7sus
B♭m9
Nev - er come to harm.
Nev - er come to harm.
E♭sus
E♭
E♭sus
E♭
G♭maj9
Here now, tak-in'
Here now,
mf
E♭m9
ease in my bod - y. Your warm
tak-in' ease in my bod - y. Your warm

A♭7sus
D♭
E♭m7
D♭m/F♭
G♭(9)
a tempo
in the bend of my arm.
in the bend of my arm.
a tempo
rit.
D♭
E♭m7
D♭m/F♭
G♭(9)
RUTH:
D♭
E♭m7
Oh, Lord, I am so tired of be - in'
D♭m/F♭
G♭(9)
D♭
E♭m7
lone - ly. Oh, Lord, I am so tired of be - in' a - fraid.
NATHAN:
Mmm

D♭m/F♭
D♭/F
G♭7
D♭7
Mmm___ Let me_ fly___ to my_ love a - cross these fields._ And I will
G♭7
D♭/F
Slowly, freely
E♭m11
a tempo
B♭m9
G♭maj9
Say hel - lo,_____ dar - lin', say, how you be.
say hel - lo,_____ dar - lin',_________ say, how you be.
colla voce
a tempo
E♭m11
D♭(9)
B♭m9
G♭maj9
B♭m(9)
G♭(9)
Light Ped.

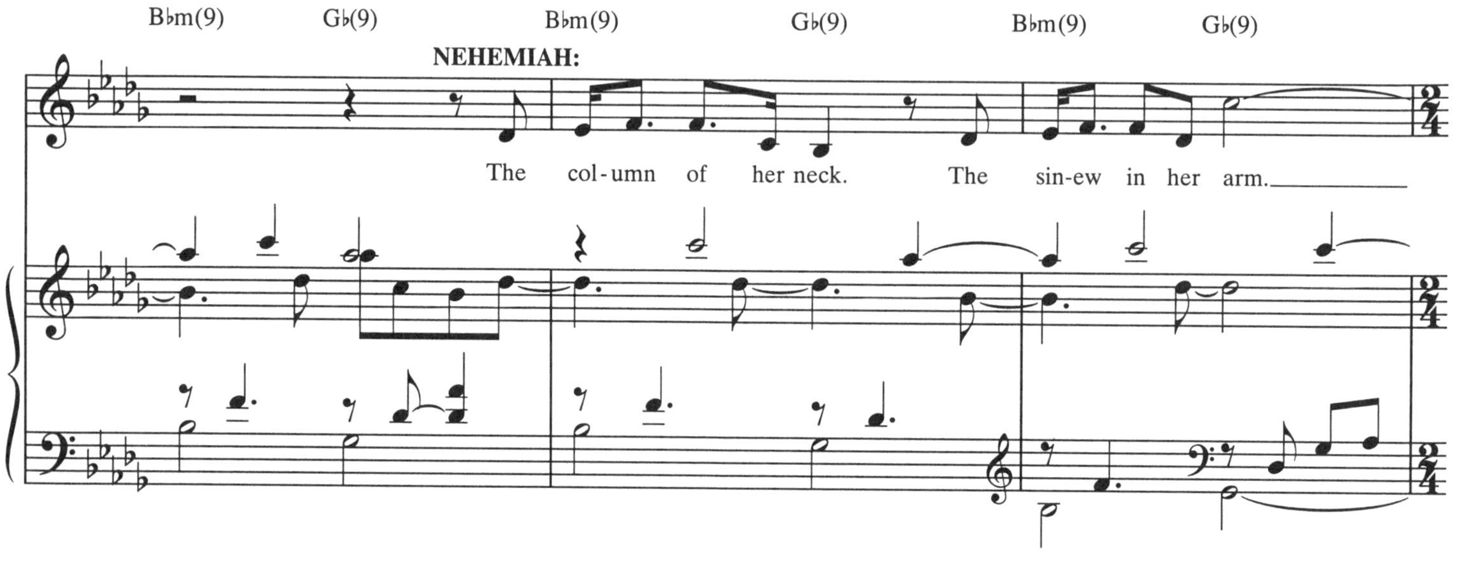
B♭m(9)
G♭(9)
B♭m(9)
G♭(9)
B♭m(9)
G♭(9)
NEHEMIAH:
The col-umn of her neck. The sin-ew in her arm.

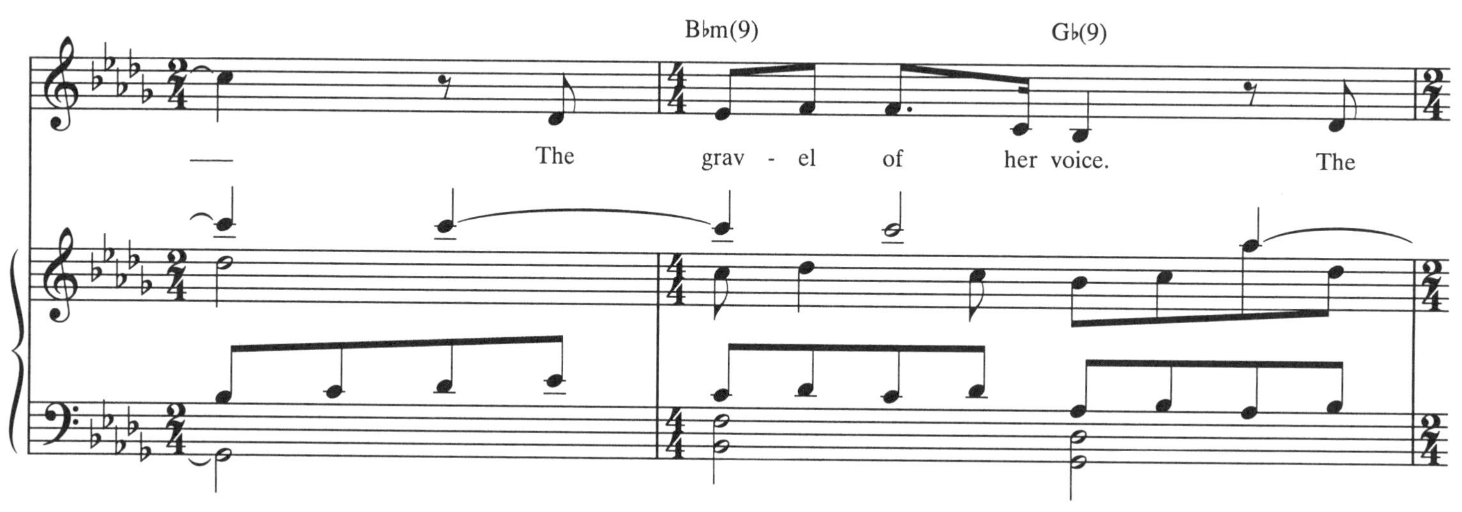
B♭m(9)
G♭(9)
The grav - el of her voice. The

B♭m(9)
Fm/A♭
G♭(9)
men-ace and the charm. I will find you a -
3

B♭sus B♭m7 G♭6/9 B♭sus B♭m7
(NEHEMIAH:)
gain. Find you some - where a - gain.
DESSA ROSE + RUTH:
mp
Taste like rain. Smell like earth.
NATHAN + KAINE:
mp
Taste like rain. Smell like earth.
f
G♭6/9 C♭maj13 B♭7sus B♭m9
(NEHEMIAH:)
Cap-ture you. You won't mock me or es-cape me or con-fuse me, Des - sa
DESSA ROSE:
Nev - er brought to harm...
RUTH, NATHAN, KAINE:
K.:
R. + N.:
Mmm Mmm
(Full)
Ped.

A alt.
(NEHEMIAH:)
Rose.
G♭maj9
DESSA ROSE:
Here now. Tak-in'
(DESSA ROSE:)
RUTH:
Here now.
(RUTH, NATHAN, KAINE:)
Ah.
NATHAN:
Here now.
KAINE:
Here now.
appassionata
mf
(DESSA ROSE:)
ease in my bod - y.
Your
(RUTH:)
Tak-in' ease in my bod - y.
Your
(NATHAN:)
Tak-in' ease in my bod - y.
Your
(KAINE:)
Tak-in' ease in my bod - y.
Your

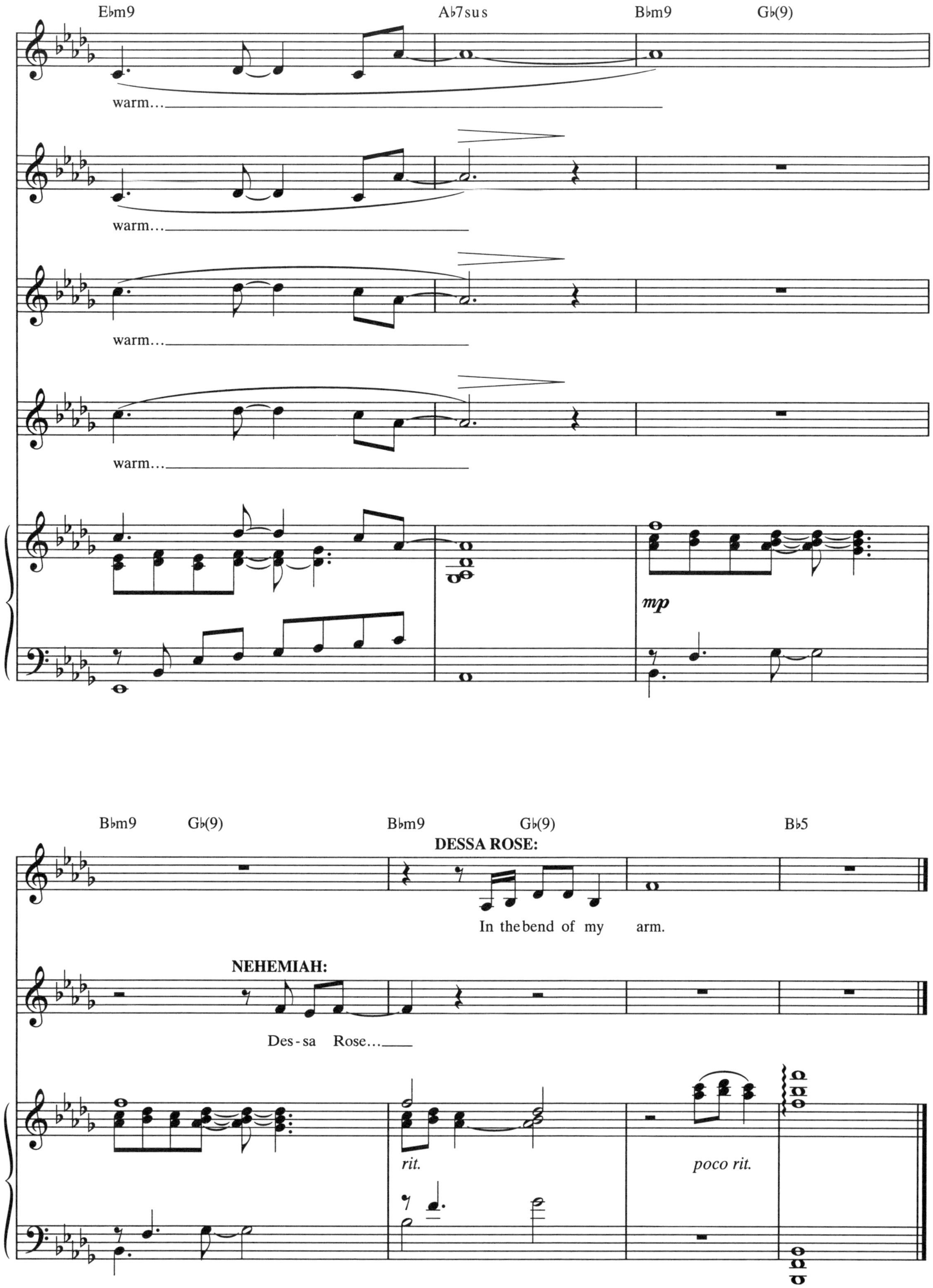

E♭m9 A♭7sus B♭m9 G♭(9)

warm…

warm…

warm…

warm…

mp

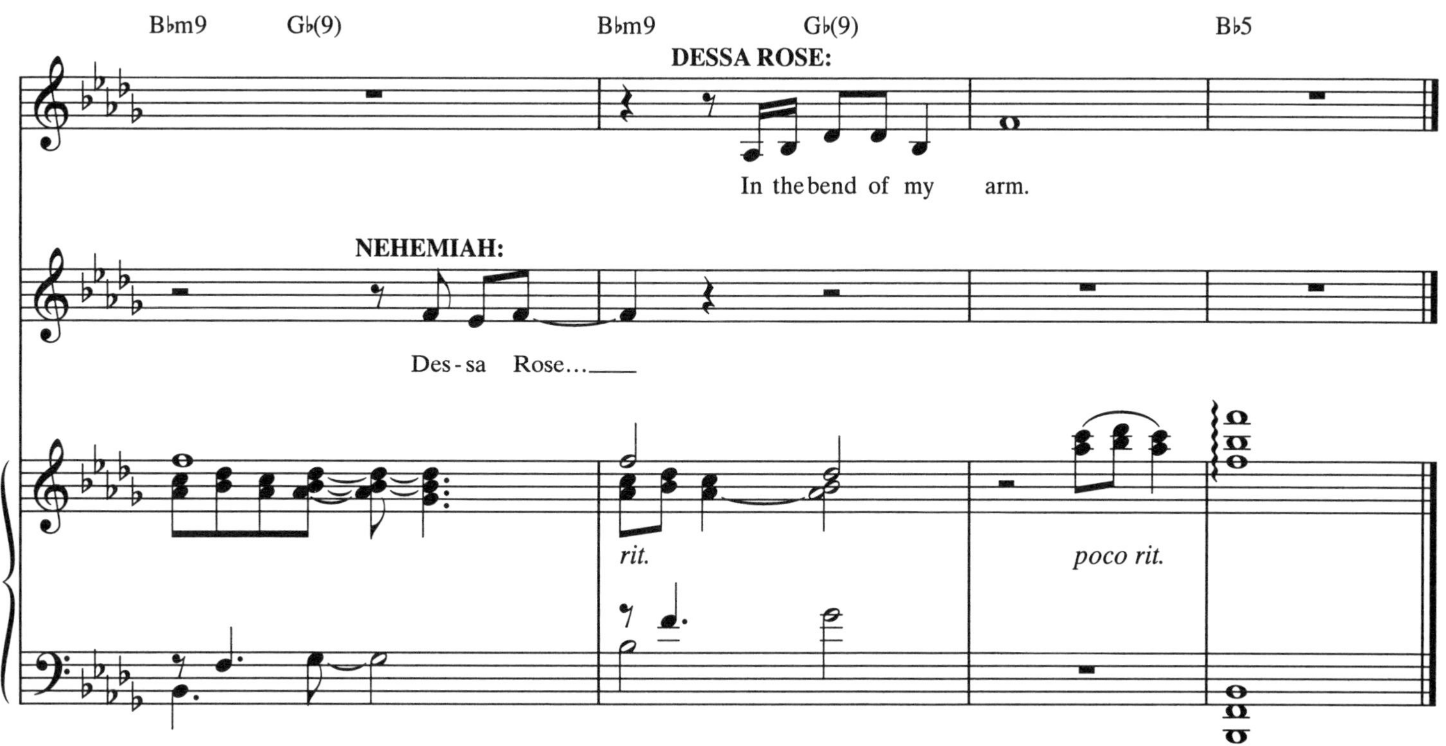

THE SCHEME

Lyrics by
LYNN AHRENS

Music by
STEPHEN FLAHERTY

Sly ragtime, not too fast (♩ = 120)
D/A
D7/C
G/B
B♭7
D/A
Bm
mf

B♭7
A7
D
A
NATHAN:
D
G7
I was won in a card__ game by a fel - la name of Crutch, And

D
B♭9
A7
A7(♯5)
D
D/C
side by side, we trav-eled man - y plac - es. Sold snake oil and e - lix - ir, pure-dee

G/B
B♭7
D/A
N.C.
A7(♯5)
D
D7
al - co - hol and such. I'd serve him drinks and slide him ex - tra a - ces. We
G7
D
A7/E
trav - eled round the Black Belt, me and Mis - ter Crutch, and by his side I learnt to steal the
D/F♯
D7
B♭7
D/A
D/C♯
Bm
D/A
hon - ey. He'd sell me off at auc - tion, *hicks* would pay too much. I'd
B♭7(♭5)
N.C.
B♭9
A7
A7(♯5)
D
D/C
run, meet up with Crutch, and split the mon - ey. He taught me how to skim a lit - tle

G/B (slide) B♭7 D/A Bm B♭7 A7 D
cream. Get sold and then you run and that's the scheme! He'd say:
D B♭7 D B♭7
Come one, come all, you up - right south - ern gents! Gath - er 'round,
D B7 B♭7 A7
look - ee here, bring your dol - lars and your cents! Got the
8va
D B♭7 D B♭7
fin - est damn nig - ger you might ev - er hope to spy. You gon'
loco

D
B7
B♭7
A7
D
kick your-self to-mor-row if you pass___ this one by.
He's a
f
D/C
G/B
Em/G
D/A
Bm
B♭
A7
prov-en buck, mul-ti-ply your stock. He can shoe, he can shine, he can mend a clock. He can
p
D
D/C
G/B
E/G♯
D/A
Bm
B♭7
A7
D
learn what-ev-er you want to teach. Got the dis-po-si-tion of a Geor-gia peach! Them
D/C
G/B
Em/G
D/A
Bm7
B♭7
A7
crack-ers all___ start wav-ing cash and, pret-ty soon,_ we've cooked their hash! Them

D
D/F♯
G
G♯dim7
A7
D
fel - las ain't yet re - al - ize. They's in for some sur - prise! 'Cause I
f
A
B♭/A
B/A
A7
wait un - til dark, off I take, o - ver the fence or 'cross the lake!
p
poco a poco cresc.
N.C.
A
D7
Worst mis - take them crack - ers make: Sold!
f
a tempo
G7
G♯dim7
Then one night he come up a-gainst a gun, hav - ing sold me twice to
sfz
mp

D/A
F♯m/C♯
Bm
some damn one. I heard some - one cry:
"Kiss your ass good - bye!"
(Spoken, imitating a stupid white person):
I may be a stupid white man, but I ain't that stupid!
(He imitates a gunshot, and simulates Mr. Crutch's death.)
N.C.
VAMP
p
Freely, reflectively with movement
E7sus
E7
G/A
A7
D
D/C
Well, I still can re - call the kind of
mf
poco rit.
mp
G/B
Gm/B♭
D/A
Bm
B♭7
A
sto - ries he would tell. He nev - er made me feel I was be - low him. He

D
D/C
G/B
B♭7
taught me I was rich with just my on - ly self to sell. I
poco rit.
a tempo
D/A
A7(♯5)
D
D7
s'pose that's 'bout the big - gest thing I owe him. We
a tempo
G7
D
D7/C
scan - da - lized the Black Belt, me and Mis - ter Crutch. We'd laugh un - til we near - ly bust a
mf
G/B
B♭7
D
D7/C
G/B
B♭7
seam. Those crack - ers nev - er met a bet - ter team. When all

D D7/C G/B E7 N.C. B♭7

— is said and done, *aw, hell,* — *we had some fun!* And that's

A7 D D7/C G/B B♭7

the scheme. — That's the

D D7/C G/B B♭7 D D7/C

scheme. — That's the scheme. —

G/B B♭7 D/A Bm B♭7 A7 D

— Get sold and then you run *and that's the scheme.*

f

WHITE MILK & RED BLOOD

Lyrics by
LYNN AHRENS

Music by
STEPHEN FLAHERTY

* Chord in ( ) indicates enharmonic spelling.

G♯m11
E(9)
G♯m7
Emaj9
F♯7sus
B
F♯/A♯
bout.
Chil-dren born
E/G♯
B/F♯
E(9)
G♯m7
C♯9
C♯m7/F♯ F♯
free or slaved.
Who we to say who lives or dies, child.
B(9)
F♯/A♯
E/G♯
(E♭/G)
D♯/F×
G♯m
E(9)
G♯m
Milk blood, we all God's chil - dren and who we to say what this
Gdim7
G♯m
B7/F♯
E(9)
G♯m
C♯m7/F♯ F♯
life's a - bout. Who we to say what this life's a -

Bsus B A2 E(9)/G♯ E6 B/D♯
bout. Now, you look at skin: cop-per or yal - low,
C♯m (E♭/G) D♯/F× G♯m C♯9 C♯m7/F♯ F♯ A2 E(9)/G♯
pink-y or sal - low or so black it seem blue. Now, you look at hair.
E6 B/D♯ G♯m7 C♯9 A9
What we care, child? Keep a head warm be it me or you.
E/F♯ F♯6 E(9)/G♯ F♯/A♯ B F♯/A♯ E/G♯ B/F♯
Hmm White milk and red blood.
sub. p
mp

E(9) G♯m7 C♯9 C♯m7/F♯ F♯ B(9) F♯/A♯
Riv - ers flow - in' and com - in' straight from God. Blood, milk, this
cresc.
mf
E/G♯ (E♭/G) D♯/F× G♯m E(9) G♯m Gdim7 G♯m B7/F♯
world keep go - in' and who we to say what this life's a - bout.
E(9) B/F♯ C♯m7/F♯ F♯
Who we to say what this life, what this life's a -
poco rit.
A6/9 E/G♯ E6/9 B/D♯ C♯7 F♯7sus B
bout. Hmm. Hmm.
mp
poco rit.

William Parry

Rachel York, LaChanze (foreground) and Company

ABOUT THE AUTHORS

Lynn Ahrens and Stephen Flaherty have been collaborators in the musical theatre since 1983.

In 1998, Ahrens and Flaherty won the theatrical triple crown-Tony Award®, Drama Desk Award and Outer Critics Circle Award for the score of the Broadway musical *Ragtime* (based on the E. L. Doctorow novel) with book by Terrence McNally. They also received Grammy® nominations for *Songs From Ragtime* and *Ragtime: Original Broadway Cast* recordings of the show. In addition, they garnered the Los Angeles Drama Critics Award for Best Score and Best Musical, and the Drama Desk, Outer Critics Circle and Drama League Awards for Best Musical. For its recent London West End premiere *Ragtime* was nominated for eight Olivier Awards including Best Musical.

Also in 1998, Ahrens and Flaherty received two Academy Award® nominations and two Golden Globe nominations for the songs and score of *Anastasia,* Twentieth Century Fox's first feature animation.

They are the co-creators of the hit Broadway musical *Once On This Island* (1990), which received eight Tony Award nominations (including Best Musical, Book and Score), NAACP Theatre Awards for Best Musical and Best Playwright, and Drama Critics Circle and Outer Critics Circle nominations. For its London West End production the show was awarded the 1995 Olivier Award as Best Musical.

They co-wrote *Seussical,* based on the works of Dr. Seuss, which premiered on Broadway in 2000 and received Grammy and Drama Desk nominations.

In addition to *Dessa Rose* they have premiered two other shows at Lincoln Center Theatre: *My Favorite Year* (1992) and *A Man of No Importance* (2002), with book by Terrence McNally, which won the 2003 Outer Critics Circle Award for Best Musical.

Their musical farce *Lucky Stiff* (1988), first produced off-Broadway by Playwrights Horizons received the Richard Rodgers Award and Washington's Helen Hayes Award as Best Musical.

Currently, they are developing two new theater works with Lincoln Center Theatre.

For the concert stage, Ahrens and Flaherty were commissioned by the Boston Pops Symphony Orchestra to create *With Voices Raised,* a piece for orchestra and mixed chorus, which has been performed and recorded at Boston's Symphony Hall and subsequently performed at Carnegie Hall in New York.

Individually, Ms Ahrens is the lyricist and co-book writer for A *Christmas Carol,* which ran for ten years at Madison Square Garden. Ms. Ahrens also wrote the teleplay of that show, which premiered on NBC in 2004 (Hallmark Entertainment). She contributed lyrics to the independent feature film *Camp* (IFC Films). For her work in network television as a songwriter, creator and producer, Ms. Ahrens has received the Emmy Award and four Emmy nominations. Her songs are a mainstay of the renowned animated series *Schoolhouse Rock.* She serves on the Board of Directors of Young Playwrights, Inc.

Mr. Flaherty wrote the incidental music for Neil Simon's play *Proposals* on Broadway. His orchestral suite, based on the musical themes of *Ragtime*, premiered at the Hollywood Bowl, and his musical themes from *Anastasia* were featured at the Bowl in a "Tribute to the Music of Twentieth Century Fox." He is a founding member of the acclaimed theatre company, Drama Dept. Upcoming projects include the musical score for Gertrude Stein's *A Long Gay Book,* directed and adapted for the stage by Frank Galati.

Cast recordings of Ahrens and Flaherty shows have been recorded by RCA/Victor, Sony, Decca Broadway, Atlantic, Varese Sarabande and JAY Records. A print anthology of their music, "The Ahrens and Flaherty Songbook," is published by Warner Chappell. Both are members of AMPAS, NARAS, ASCAP, serve on the Dramatists Guild Council and co-chair the Jonathan Larson Musical Theatre Fellows Program at the Dramatists Guild.

Stephen Flaherty and Lynn Ahrens

If you are interested in obtaining information on the performing rights for Ahrens and Flaherty shows, please contact:

Peter Franklin
The William Morris Agency
1325 Avenue of the Americas
New York, NY 10019
(212) 903-1550
pf@wma.com

For information on the stock and amateur rights for any of their shows, please contact:

Music Theatre International (MTI)
421 West 54th Street, 2nd Floor
New York, NY 10019
(212) 541-4684
licensing@mtishows.com
www.mtishows.com